Workbook

WORLD ENGLISH1

Real People • Real Places • Real Language

Kristin L. Johannsen

HEINLE
CENGAGE Learning™

Australia • Brazil • Japan • Korea • Mexico • Singapore • Spain • United Kingdom • United States

HEINLE
CENGAGE Learning™

World English 1 Workbook
Real People • Real Places • Real Language
Kristin L. Johannsen

Publisher: Jason Mann

Commissioning Editor: Carol Goodwright

Development Editor: Louisa Essenhigh

Technology Development Manager: Debie Mirtle

Director of Global Marketing: Ian Martin

Product Manager: Ruth McAleavey

Content Project Editor: Amy Smith

ELT Production Controller: Denise Power

Cover Designer: Page 2 LLC

Compositor: MPS Limited, A Macmillan Company

Head of Production and Manufacturing: Alissa Chappell

ISBN: 978-1-111-21766-2

Heinle, Cengage Learning
Cheriton House
North Way
Andover
Hampshire
SP10 5BE
United Kingdom

Cengage Learning is a leading provider of customized learning solutions with office locations around the globe, including Singapore, the United Kingdom, Australia, Mexico, Brazil, and Japan. Locate your local office at: **international.cengage.com/region**

Cengage Learning products are represented in Canada by Nelson Education, Ltd.

Visit Heinle online at **elt.heinle.com**

Visit our corporate website at **www.cengage.com**

Cover Image: Sergio Amiti/National Geographic Image Collection, Menara Gardens, Marrakech

Printed in China
3 4 5 6 7 8 9 10 – 15 14 13 12 11

CONTENTS

Scope and Sequence 4

Unit 1   People 7

Unit 2   Work, Rest, and Play 13

Unit 3   Going Places 19

Unit 4   Food 25

Unit 5   Sports 31

Unit 6   Destinations 37

Unit 7   Communication 43

Unit 8   The Future 49

Unit 9   Shopping for Clothes 55

Unit 10   Lifestyles 61

Unit 11   Achievements 67

Unit 12   Consequences 73

Vocabulary Index 79

SCOPE AND SEQUENCE

	Grammar	Vocabulary	Communication	Reading and Writing
People page 7				
UNIT 1	*Be* Simple present tense Personal pronouns	Professions Nationalities Descriptive adjectives (opposites)	Asking and answering questions about personal information	"The World of Work" Describing a person's job
Work, Rest, and Play page 13				
UNIT 2	Simple present tense Prepositions of time (*in, on, at*) Adverbs of frequency	Everyday activities Celebrations	Talking about everyday routines	"Happy New Year!" Describing a favorite celebration
Going Places page 19				
UNIT 3	Possession Imperatives *Should* for advice	Travel Travel documents	Filling out forms Rising and falling intonation	"Travel Light!" Writing about packing a bag
Food page 25				
UNIT 4	Count and non-count nouns *Some, any* *How much, how many* *Lots of, a few, a little*	Food	Ordering meals at a restaurant	"Colcannon from Ireland" Writing about a famous local food
Sports page 31				
UNIT 5	Present continuous tense Simple present tense vs. present continuous tense	Sports	Describing present time activities	"Sports Around the World" Writing about a popular sport
Destinations page 37				
UNIT 6	Simple past tense (regular and irregular verbs) *Was, were*	Vacation travel Descriptive adjectives	Talking about a vacation	A letter from a friend Writing a letter to a friend

	Grammar	Vocabulary	Communication	Reading and Writing
Communication page 43				
UNIT 7	Object pronouns Linking verbs	Methods of communication Sensory adjectives	Giving contact information	"How do animals communicate?" Writing about personal communication
The Future page 49				
UNIT 8	*Going to* for future plans *Going to* and *will* for predictions	Short- and long-term plans Weather and accessories	Expressing personal plans Making predictions about the weather	"Education for Tomorrow" Writing predictions about schools in the future
Shopping for Clothes page 55				
UNIT 9	Comparative adjectives Superlative adjectives	Clothing Caring for clothes Clothing materials	Shopping for clothes	"The Coolest T-Shirts in the World" Writing about favorite everyday clothes
Lifestyles page 61				
UNIT 10	Modals for advice Questions with *how*	Healthy and unhealthy habits Compound adjectives	Giving advice	"How Long Will You Live?" Writing about changing a personal habit
Achievements page 67				
UNIT 11	Present perfect tense Present perfect tense vs. simple past tense	Chores and everyday tasks Lifetime achievements	Assessing job qualifications Making a recommendation	"Amazing Achievements: Stephen Hawking" Writing about what you have done to improve your English
Consequences page 73				
UNIT 12	Real conditionals	Money and finances Animals and habitats	Describing consequences Giving financial advice	"Nature Vacations" Writing about the best and worst vacation spots for the environment

CREDITS

ILLUSTRATION

8: Ted Hammond/IllustrationOnline.com; **10:** Jim Atherton; **13:** (all) Mark Collins/IllustrationOnline.com; **17, 20:** Jim Atherton; **25:** Ted Hammond/Illustration Online.com; **29:** (all) Jim Atherton; **44:** Nesbitt Graphics, Inc.; **51:** Jim Atherton; **58:** Nesbitt Graphics, Inc.; **67:** Ted Hammond/IllustrationOnline.com; **68:** Nesbitt Graphics, Inc.; **73:** (1, 2) Keith Neely/IllustrationOnLine.com, (3) Jim Atherton, (4) Keith Neely/ IllustrationOnline.com; **76:** Nesbitt Graphics, Inc.

PHOTO

7: (t, l to r) Sandra Nicol/iStockphoto, Gerenme/iStockphoto, Stephen Coburn/Shutterstock, (1m, l to r) Diana Lundin/iStockphoto, Photodisc/ Getty Images, (2m, l to r) Margo Silver/Getty Images, Rich Legg/ iStockphoto, AVAVA/Shutterstock, (b) Celso Diniz/Shutterstock; **9:** (t) Sean Locke/iStockphoto, (m) Ramzi Hachicho/Shutterstock, (b) Goodshoot/ JupiterImages; **10:** (l to r) George F. Mobley/National Geographic Image Collection, Wilfried Krecichwost/Getty Images, Stephen Coburn/ Shutterstock, Photo and Co/Getty Images; **11:** David Boyer/National Geographic Image Collection; **12:** PhotostoGo.com; **13:** Magda L/Dreamstime; **14:** Sergei Bachlakov/Shutterstock; **15:** (1) Gino Santa Maria/ iStockphoto, (2) Diane Diederich/iStockphoto, (3) PhotostoGo.com, (4) Nasser Bu-hamad/Dreamstime, (5) Nasser Bu-hamad/Dreamstime, (6) photos.com; **16:** (tl) Gertjan Hooijer/iStockphoto, (tr) Roger Parkes/ Alamy, (b) blue jean images/Getty Images; **18:** Yuri Arcurs/Shutterstock; **19:** (t) Yuliya Trukhan/Dreamstime, (1) AVAVA/Shutterstock, (2) Stephen Coburn/Shutterstock, (3) Jennifer Trenchard/iStockphoto, (4) Emmanuel Faure/Getty Images, (5) James Cotier/Getty Images, (6) Blend Images/Getty Images; **21:** (l to r) Paul Cowan/Dreamstime, photos.com, iStockphoto, Brian A Jackson/Shutterstock, Richard Cano/iStockphoto; **22:** (t) PhotostoGo.com, (b) iStockphoto; **24:** egd/Shutterstock; **26:** Blend Images/ Jupiter Images; **27:** (1) OlgaLis/Shutterstock, (2) Mike Grindley/Shutterstock, (3) OSVALDRU/Shutterstock, (4) Dan Peretz/Shutterstock, (5) Aaron Amat/Shutterstock, (6) Oliver Hoffmann/Shutterstock, (7) Viktorfischer/ Dreamstime, (8) Natalia7/Shutterstock, (m) Tony Wear/Shutterstock, (b) Sparkling Moments Photography/Shutterstock; **28:** Amanda Heywood/ age fotostock; **30:** iStockphoto; **31:** (1) Eric Michaud/iStockphoto, (2) Galina Barskaya/Shutterstock, (3) Jakub Cejpek/Dreamstime, (4) Jenny Hill/ iStockphoto, (5) Monkey Business Images/Dreamstime, (6) Benis Arapovic/ Shutterstock; **32:** (l to r) PhotostoGo.com, Paul Clarke/Shutterstock, iStockphoto, Joanne Green/iStockphoto, Ivan Josifovic/Shutterstock, iStockphoto; **33:** (1) Denis Pepin/Shutterstock, (2) Andresr/Shutterstock, (3) iStockphoto, (4) Mike Flippo/Shutterstock, (5) Coquilleau/Shutterstock, (6) Susan McGinty/iStockphoto, (7) Sherry Schuller/iStockphoto, (8) Ruslan Gilmanshin/iStockphoto; **34:** (t to b) Ruslan Gilmanshin/iStockphoto, Andre Ringuette/NHLI via Getty Images, Todd Taulman/Shutterstock, Galina Barskaya/Dreamstime, Mikhail Kokhanchikov/Dreamstime, Andrew Penner/ iStockphoto; **36:** Mike Flippo/Shutterstock; **37:** (l) Evan Meyer/Shutterstock (r) Maceofoto/iStockphoto; **38:** (tl) Michael Mattox/iStockphoto, (tr) Keith Levit/Shutterstock, (bl) iStockphoto, (br) lexan/Shutterstock; **39:** (1) Renee Lee/iStockphoto, (2) Celso Pupo Rodrigues/Dreamstime, (3) Viorika Prikhodko/iStockphoto; **40:** Christian Wheatley/Dreamstime; **41:** (t) Chris Sargent/Shutterstock, (m) johnnychaos/Shutterstock, (b) iStockphoto; **42:** Sean Nel/Dreamstime; **43:** (1) Monkey Business Images/Dreamstime, (2) Andres Rodriguez/Shutterstock, (3) Timurpix/Shutterstock, (4) Susan Law Cain/Dreamstime, (5) Mikhail Nekrasov/Dreamstime; **45:** (1) Alexander Motrenko/Shutterstock, (2) Shailesh Nanal/Dreamstime, (3) iStockphoto, (4) Jack Hollingsworth/Dreamstime, (5) Paul Roux/iStockphoto; **46:** (t) photos.com, (m) Ewan Chesser/Shutterstock, (b) Pauline S Mills/ iStockphoto; **47:** (l) Irving N Saperstein/iStockphoto, (m) Iurii Konoval/ Shutterstock, (r) Jon Larson/iStockphoto; **48:** Fotolistic/Shutterstock; **49:** (l) Rmarmion/Dreamstime, (r) Elena Elisseeva/Dreamstime; **50:** Chris Schmidt/ iStockphoto; **52:** (t) Noam Armonn/Dreamstime, (m) letty17/Shutterstock, (bl) Catherine Yeulet/iStockphoto, (br) Xinhua/Landov; **53:** (l) Gary Walts/ Syracuse Newspapers/The Image Works, (m) Rob Marmion/Shutterstock, (r) Michael Jung/Shutterstock; **54:** Svlumagraphica/Dreamstime; **55:** (1) Monika Adamczyk/iStockphoto, (2) photos.com, (3) Juri Semjonow/ iStockphoto, (4) Anton Gvozdikov/iStockphoto, (5) photos.com, (6) Keith Webber Jr./iStockphoto, (7) Mark Fairey/iStockphoto, (8) Igor Terekhov/ iStockphoto, (9) Jill Chen/iStockphoto, (10) Zoran Kolundzija/iStockphoto, (11) Vincent Birlouez/iStockphoto, (12) Mazzzur/Shutterstock; **56:** Simone van den Berg/Shutterstock; **57:** (1) Graça Victoria/iStockphoto, (2) Nancy Louie/iStockphoto, (3) Sandra Cunningham/Shutterstock, (4) iStockphoto, (5) Frances Twitty/iStockphoto; **58:** Nick D/Shutterstock; **60:** Boris Stroujko/ Shutterstock; **61:** Andres Rodriguez/Dreamstime; **62:** (t) Willie B. Thomas/ iStockphoto, (m) Spauln/Dreamstime, (b) dellison/Shutterstock; **63:** Flynt/ Dreamstime; **64:** (t to b) Chrissie Shepherd/Dreamstime, Galina Barskaya/ Shutterstock, Constantin Opris/Dreamstime, Photoroller/Dreamstime, Diego Cervo/Shutterstock; **66:** Sunflowerhike/Dreamstime; **67:** Yuriy Brykaylo/Dreamstime; **68:** (t) Andrzej Podsiad/Dreamstime, (b) Yuri Arcurs/ Shutterstock; **69:** Mandy Godbehear/Dreamstime; **70:** Chris Davies/ ArenaPAL/Topham/The Image Works; **71:** NASA/Lightroom/Topham/ The Image Works; **72:** Ian Poole/Dreamstime; **74:** Andres Rodriguez/ Dreamstime; **75:** (1) Seleznev Oleg/Shutterstock, (2) EcoPrint/Shutterstock, (3) Ian Scott/Shutterstock, (4) djbp/Shutterstock, (5) photos.com; **76:** (t) Roy Hsu/Getty Images, (m) Steve Froebe/iStockphoto, (b) Piotr Sikora/ Shutterstock; **77:** (tl) Paul Clarke/Shutterstock, (tr) Steve Rosset/iStockphoto, (b) Pichugin Dmitry/Shutterstock; **78:** photos.com.

Lesson A

A. Unscramble the job titles. Complete the sentences.

(hpootragephr) 1. He's a __photographer__.

(fceh) 2. He's a _____.

(ginreeen) 3. She's an _____.

(rotcdo) 4. She's a _____.

(icelop fofcire) 5. She's a _____.

(tolpi) 6. She's a _____.

(lervta getna) 7. He's a _____.

(chaetre) 8. He's a _____.

B. Write the nationality.

1. France __French__

2. Jordan _____

3. Bahrain _____

4. Thailand _____

5. Australia _____

6. Peru _____

7. Mexico _____

8. Your nationality: _____

C. Read the conversation. Write the pronouns and the correct form of *be*.

Cristina: Where (1) are __you__ from, Mary?

Mary: (2) _____ from Australia.

Cristina: So, (3) _____ Australian. Sounds cool. (4) _____ from Sydney?

Mary: Yes, I am. And you, Cristina? (5) _____ Mexican?

Cristina: No, (6) _____. (7) _____ Brazilian.

Mary: Wow! Brazil. I'd love to go to Brazil. Which city (8) _____ from?

Cristina: (9) _____ from Rio de Janeiro. (10) _____ a cool city!

Lesson B

A. *What's My Name?* is a TV show. Read the information and complete the sentences.

Name: Anita	Name: Isabel	Name: Carmen
Age: 23	Age: 25	Age: 25
Nationality: Mexican	Nationality: Chilean	Nationality: Mexican
City: Puebla	City: Santiago	City: Mexico City
Job: travel agent	Job: travel agent	Job: nurse

Contestant: (1) __Are you_____ a travel agent?

Woman #1: (2) _____, I am.

Contestant: And (3) _____ Chilean?

Woman #1: No, (4) _____.

Contestant: Hmm. So, you're Mexican.

Woman #1: Yes, (5) _____.

Contestant: Are you 23 (6) _____?

Woman #1: Yes!

Contestant: Is (7) _____ Anita?

Woman #1: Yes! You're right!

Contestant: Are you Mexican?

Woman #2: Yes, (8) _____.

Contestant: (9) _____ 25 years old?

Woman #2: Yes.

Contestant: Are you a travel agent?

Woman #2: No, (10) _____.

Contestant: So, (11) _____ a nurse?

Woman #2: Yes. You're right.

Contestant: Is your name Carmen?

Woman #2: Yes, (12) _____!

B. Write the contractions.

1. I am __I'm_____
2. she is _____
3. it is _____
4. you are _____
5. is not _____
6. he is _____
7. they are _____
8. we are _____
9. are not _____

Lesson C

A. Match the opposites.

1. good __b__
2. rich ___
3. boring ___
4. happy ___
5. dangerous ___
6. difficult ___

   a. easy
   b. bad
   c. safe
   d. poor
   e. unhappy
   f. interesting

B. Complete the sentences about jobs. Use your ideas.

1. Her job is dangerous. She's __a pilot_____.
2. His job is interesting. He's _____.
3. Her job is boring. She's _____.
4. His job is difficult. He's _____.
5. Her job is easy. She's _____.
6. My job is _____. I'm _____.

C. Complete the sentences with possessive adjectives (*my*, *your*, *his*, *her*, *their*).

1. Hello! _____ name is Asma.
2. Ms. Costa is a photographer. _____ job is very interesting.
3. They're my brothers. _____ names are Ali and Hassan.
4. You're a nurse! Is _____ job difficult?
5. I like my teacher. _____ name is Mr. Clark.
6. Mr. Shen likes _____ job. He's an engineer.
7. I'm very happy. I like _____ new job.

D. Unscramble the questions. Then write your answers.

1. (your what name is) _____?
   _____.

2. (from you are where) _____?
   _____.

3. (you what do do) _____?
   _____.

4. (work is your interesting) _____?
   _____.

5. (your is easy work) _____?
   _____.

The World of Work

Today, many people go to work in new countries. Here, four of these people talk about their jobs.

Michael Murphy is a doctor. He's from Ireland, but he works in many countries. He says, "My work is sometimes dangerous, but it's always interesting. I love helping people."

Shaukat Ali is a taxi driver in London, England. He's from Pakistan. He says, "I love my job! It's difficult, because London is so big. But the people are very nice."

Natsuko Mori is from Osaka, Japan. She works in Brazil now. She says, "I'm a teacher in a language school. I teach Japanese to Brazilian students. My students are very good, and I like my job."

Moses Agba is a soccer player from Nigeria, in Africa. Now he plays for a team in Italy. He says, "People think my job is exciting. That's true, but it isn't easy. I like living in Italy, but it's very cold here."

A. Read the sentences. Circle **T** for *true* or **F** for *false*.

1. Natsuko is Brazilian.   T   F
2. Shaukat works in a car.   T   F
3. Playing soccer is an easy job.   T   F
4. Michael's job is dangerous.   T   F
5. These people like their jobs.   T   F

B. Write the person's name. You can repeat names.

1. _____ is Japanese.
2. _____ lives in Italy.
3. _____ works with students.
4. _____ has a dangerous job.
5. _____ works in a big city.
6. _____ is Irish.
7. _____ has an exciting job.

C. Look at the picture. Write sentences about Lina and her job. Use your ideas.

_____

_____

_____

_____

_____

_____

_____

_____

_____

_____

Review

Solve the crossword puzzle with vocabulary and grammar from this unit.

Across

4. not safe
7. not poor
8. He's from Canada. He's _____.
11. I'm from Mexico. I'm _____.
14. not easy
15. not interesting
17. They _____ students.

Down

1. She's from France. She's _____.
2. They're from Korea. They're _____.
3. I have a brother. ___ name is Iqbal.
5. job
6. He's from Thailand. He's _____.
9. I _____ an engineer.
10. A _____ works in a school.
11. I like ___ job because it's exciting.
12. A _____ works in an airplane.
13. I'm _____ Bahrain.
16. My name _____ Elisa.

Lesson A

A. Match the columns to make activities.

1. read **j**   a. work
2. get ___   b. the bus
3. eat ___   c. breakfast
4. go ___   d. out
5. take ___   e. TV
6. catch ___   f. up
7. go to ___   g. nap
8. take a ___   h. to bed
9. watch ___   i. a shower
10. visit ___   j. the newspaper
11. start ___   k. friends
12. eat ___   l. the park

B. What do you do every day? Write activities from exercise **A**.

get up, _____

_____

C. Complete the sentences with prepositions of time (*in*, *on*, *at*).

1. Mark gets up _____ 4:00 _____ the morning. He's a policeman.
2. In my country, people take a shower _____ the evening.
3. I visit my friends _____ Sunday.
4. Katie works _____ weekends. She's a nurse.
5. Our English class is _____ 2:30 _____ the afternoon.
6. Do you go to school _____ Saturday?

D. Look at the pictures and write sentences about Elvin.

1. _____

2. _____

3. _____

4. _____

Lesson B

A. You are a guest on a TV program called *Everyday Life*. Unscramble the questions. Then write your answers.

1. have what breakfast you time do **What time do you have breakfast** ?

_____

2. what the do you in evening do _____ ?

_____

3. have do restaurant dinner you in a _____ ?

_____

4. free time you do what do in your _____ ?

_____

5. you what Saturdays do do on _____ ?

_____

6. do sports like you _____ ?

_____

7. what you do on do weekends _____ ?

_____

8. do the go to mall you _____ ?

_____

B. Think about a person in your family. What does he or she do on Friday? Complete the chart.

Name: _____

Friday morning	He/She _____
Friday afternoon	
Friday evening	

Lesson C

A. Label the pictures.

celebrate   fireworks   costume   mask   present   decorate

1. _____   2. _____   3. _____

4. _____   5. _____   6. _____

B. Write the adverbs of frequency on the line. | usually   never   sometimes   always   often |

0 percent   100 percent

C. Write the sentences again using the adverbs of frequency.

1. I eat breakfast at home. (usually)

   _____

2. American Independence Day is on July 4. (always)

   _____

3. We work on New Year's Day. (never)

   _____

4. It is cold in December. (usually)

   _____

5. We give presents to our friends. (often)

   _____

D. Write sentences about things you do.

1. (never) _I never_____ .

2. (always) _____ .

3. (sometimes) _____ .

Happy New Year!

In the Netherlands, New Year's Day is always on January 1. It's very cold, so people stay home, and they clean their houses. They have a party with their friends, and they eat special food like donuts. In the evening, they watch a funny TV program about the old year, and then they have fireworks.

In Iran, New Year's Day isn't in January. It's called Nowruz, and it's in March. People always buy new clothes and clean their houses. They make special food, like meat and rice. They visit all the people in their families and give them presents. It's a very busy time!

Chinese New Year is in January or February. The date is different every year. It's a big celebration for 15 days. People don't go to work. They clean their houses and send cards to their friends. They eat a big dinner with their families, and they give presents and money to all the children. At night, they watch fireworks.

A. Which country is it? Check ✓ the answers. You can have one, two, or three answers.

New Year's Day celebrations	The Netherlands	Iran	China
1. People eat special food.			
2. People watch fireworks.			
3. It's in January.			
4. People give presents.			
5. It's a long celebration.			
6. People watch TV.			
7. People clean their houses.			

B. Complete the sentences. Use your ideas.

1. On New Year's Day, I _____
    _____.

2. I would like to celebrate New Year's Day in (the Netherlands/Iran/China) because
    _____.

C. Write about your favorite celebration. What do people do then?

_____

_____

_____

_____

_____

_____

_____

_____

Review

Solve the crossword puzzle with vocabulary and grammar from this unit.

Across

3. She always ___ to bed at eleven o'clock.
6. He always ___ a shower at eight o'clock.
7. I ___ the bus at nine thirty.
9. We give ___ to our friends at New Year.
11. I go to work ___ the morning.
12. In my ___ time, I play sports.
13. We usually ___ breakfast at home.
15. You cover your face with a ___.
16. I see my family ___ Friday.

Down

1. She ___ her friends on Saturdays.
2. I never ___ TV.
4. I sometimes ___ a nap.
5. People ___ their houses with lights.
7. special clothes for a festival
8. a time to do special things
10. We sometimes eat ___ in restaurants.
12. We have ___ on special days.
14. I get up ___ seven o'clock.

Lesson A

A. What are the steps in a trip? Fill in the correct verb in each sentence. You can use the verbs again.

| claim take check buy pack go |

1. You _____ your ticket from a travel agent.
2. You _____ your bags at home before your trip.
3. You _____ a taxi to go to the airport.
4. You _____ in when you get to the airport.
5. You take off your coat when you _____ through security.
6. Sometimes you _____ duty-free goods in a shop at the airport.
7. You _____ one small bag when you board the airplane.
8. You _____ your baggage at the baggage carousel.
9. Officers look in your passport when you _____ through immigration.
10. Custom officials look in your bag when you _____ through customs.

B. Whose bag is this? Write three sentences about each picture.

1.
  a. **It's my bag.** _____.
  b. **It belongs to me.** _____.
  c. **It's mine.** _____.

2.
  a. **It's your** _____.
  b. _____.
  c. _____.

3.
  a. **It's** _____.
  b. _____.
  c. _____.

4.
  a. _____.
  b. _____.
  c. _____.

5.
  a. **It's our bag.** _____.
  b. _____.
  c. _____.

6.
  a. _____.
  b. _____.
  c. _____.

Lesson B

A. Match the questions and answers.

1. Is this your first time in our country? ___
2. Where are you staying? ___
3. Is this your bag? ___
4. Can I see your passport please? ___
5. Can I see your ticket please? ___
6. What is the purpose of your visit? ___
7. Window or aisle? ___

   a. Yes. Here it is.
   b. I'd like a window seat.
   c. I have an e-ticket. Here's the number.
   d. No. I was here last year.
   e. At the Grand Hotel.
   f. I'm here on vacation.
   g. No, it isn't. The brown bag is mine.

B. Claudia Torres is traveling to Bertastan (a fictitious island country) for her vacation. Complete the immigration form with her information.

| Argentinean | July 1, 1988 | Claudia | Buenos Aires | Metro City |
| Paradise Hotel, 118 Beach Road, Metro City | | Argentina | | Torres |

REPUBLIC OF BERTASTAN Immigration Form
1. Family name:
2. First name:
3. Date of birth:
4. Place of birth:
5. Nationality:
6. Country of residence:
7. Destination in this country:
8. Hotel address:

C. Mark the rising and falling tone in the sentences with ↗ and ↘. Then say the sentences out loud.

1. Let's visit New York, Boston, and Miami.

2. Here are my passport, visa, and ticket.

3. Every morning, I get up, take a shower, and read the newspaper.

4. We're going to Egypt, Jordan, Syria and Turkey.

5. You can have coffee, tea, milk, or juice.

6. In the evening, I eat dinner, do my homework, and watch TV.

Lesson C

A. Unscramble the words.

1. This has your name and photo in it: (ssporpta) _____
2. You use this card to buy things: (dercti drac) _____
3. You need this to enter a country: (svai) _____
4. You show this to get on an airplane: (leinria icktte) _____
5. This is a kind of money for traveling: (svarterle cksech) _____
6. You need this to drive a car in other countries: (rentnilatioan verdirs censile) _____

   _____

7. You use this money every day: (hasc) _____
8. You need this if you get sick: (vartle sniruacen) _____
9. You write this to pay for something: (khcce) _____

B. Write advice about these things for travelers in your country. Use imperatives.

1. **Don't bring a lot of cash. It isn't safe.** _____
2. _____
3. _____
4. _____
5. _____

C. Unscramble the questions. Write answers about your country with *should* or *shouldn't*.

1. rent I a car should _____?

   You _____ because _____

   _____.

2. I a warm coat should take _____?

   You _____ because _____

   _____.

3. should insurance get travel I _____?

   You _____ because _____

   _____.

4. should I take lots of money _____?

   You _____ because _____

   _____.

Travel *Light!*

Even on a long trip, you don't need a lot of heavy suitcases. You need only two bags—a carry-on bag and a check-in bag. Here are some pointers for packing them.

Carry-on bag

- Your carry-on bag should be small and light.
- The most important things for your trip (passport, plane tickets, traveler's checks, credit cards, keys, etc.) should go in your carry-on bag.
- Bring snacks to eat on the plane. Cookies, nuts, and dried fruit are good. Don't bring chocolate—it's very messy. For long trips, bring a sandwich. And don't bring water—it's heavy and you can get it at the airport.
- Remember to bring a good book or some magazines to read.

Check-in bag

- Your check-in bag should be strong.
- Your clothes, shoes, and other everyday things should go in your check-in bag.
- Make a list to help you remember everything.
- Pack your bag early—don't pack on the same day as your trip!
- Think about the weather. Do you need a coat and gloves, or t-shirts and shorts? Choose the right clothes! Pack your clothes inside plastic bags.
- Put your name and your hotel's address and telephone number on your bag. Put this information inside the bag too.

Have a great trip!

A. Answer true or false. Circle **T** for *true* or **F** for *false*.

1. You need three bags to go on a trip.   T   F
2. Your carry-on bag should be big and strong.   T   F
3. Your carry-on bag is for things you need on the airplane.   T   F
4. Your check-in bag is for clothes and things you use on your vacation.   T   F
5. You should put your home address on your check-in bag.   T   F

B. Are these things good ideas or bad ideas?

	good idea	bad idea
1. packing your bag a few days before your trip		
2. putting your keys in your carry-on bag		
3. getting information about the weather before you pack		
4. packing chocolate in your check-in bag		
5. bringing water in your bags		
6. putting your name on your bags		
7. bringing a sandwich with you		
8. putting your credit card in your carry-on bag		

C. What do you pack in your bags for a trip? Why?

_____

_____

_____

_____

_____

_____

_____

_____

_____

_____

_____

_____

Review

Solve the crossword puzzle with vocabulary and grammar from this unit.

Across

2. It's their car. It belongs to __.
3. I __ my bags in the morning.
9. It's his book. It belongs to __.
10. Show your passport at __.
11. You __ bring a sweater. It's a good idea.
13. It's your ticket. It's __.
14. __ house is it? It's Omar's.

Down

1. You need a __ to go into this country.
2. I always __ a taxi to the airport.
3. an ID with your name and photo
4. You buy things with a __ card.
5. You go __ security at the airport.
6. It's my bag. It's __.
7. You need an international driver's __ to rent a car.
8. You need travel __ if you get sick.
12. __ bring cash. It's not safe!
15. It's our car. It's __.

Lesson A

A. Write the names of the foods on the lines.

1. _____   5. _____   9. _____   13. _____

2. _____   6. _____   10. _____   14. _____

3. _____   7. _____   11. _____   15. _____

4. _____   8. _____   12. _____

B. Look at the picture in exercise **A**. What's in the kitchen? Complete the sentences with *a*, *an*, *some*, or *any*.

1. We have _____ cheese.

2. There isn't _____ soda.

3. Do we have _____ coffee?

4. We need _____ tomato for the salad.

5. There aren't _____ lemons.

6. We have _____ bananas.

7. We don't have _____ green peppers.

8. There is _____ juice.

C. What's in your kitchen now? Write sentences about food.

1. _____

2. _____

3. _____

4. _____

Lesson B

A. A waiter and a customer are in a restaurant. Unscramble the sentences in their conversation.

1. (are order ready you to)

    Waiter: _____?

2. (recommend what you would)

    Customer: _____?

3. (excellent the chicken is)

    Waiter: _____.

4. (come does chicken with salad the)

    Customer: _____?

5. (does yes it)

    Waiter: _____.

6. (a baked potato have I'll the and chicken)

    Customer: _____.

7. (like would else you anything)

    Waiter: _____?

8. (like I a glass of would mineral water)

    Customer: _____.

B. Read the menu. Write a new conversation. Use your ideas.

Main Dishes	*Side Dishes*
Lemon Chicken Half a chicken in lemon sauce, served with rice	Green salad Tomato salad Vegetable soup Onion soup
Fried Fish Three pieces of fish, served with fried potatoes	*Drinks* Cola Mineral water
Italian Meatballs Two large meatballs, served with spaghetti and tomato sauce	Coffee Tea

Waiter: _____

You: _____

Waiter: _____

You: _____

Waiter: _____

You: _____

Waiter: _____

You: _____

Lesson C

A. Label the foods.

1. _____
2. _____
3. _____
4. _____

5. _____
6. _____
7. _____
8. _____

B. What should these people eat? Write foods from Lesson **A** and Lesson **C** and your own ideas. Use *lots of*, *a few*, or *a little*.

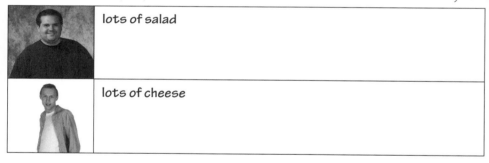

	lots of salad
	lots of cheese

C. Write questions with *How much* or *How many*.

1. DVDs **How many DVDs do you have?** _____
2. books _____
3. money _____
4. time _____
5. good friends _____

D. Answer the questions in exercise **C**. Write answers that are true for you. Use *lots of*, *a few*, or *a little*.

1. **I have lots of DVDs.** _____
2. _____
3. _____
4. _____
5. _____

International Recipes:
Colcannon from Ireland

People in Ireland like to eat this dish in cold weather.

Ingredients:

500 grams of cabbage
4 large potatoes
2 onions
½ cup of milk
salt
pepper
butter

Step 1 Cut the cabbage in large pieces. Put it in a pan with a little water and boil it for 10 minutes. Pour out the water.

Step 2 Cut the potatoes in pieces. Boil them in water for 15 minutes. The potatoes should be very soft. Pour out the water. Add salt and pepper and mash the potatoes.

Step 3 Cut 2 onions into small pieces. Cook them in ½ cup of milk for 10 minutes.

Step 4 In a large pan, mix the milk and onions with the potatoes. Then add the cabbage. Cook until it is hot.

Step 5 Put the hot colcannon in a large bowl. Add pieces of butter on top.

A. Write the numbers of the steps in the recipe below the pictures.

_____ _____ _____

_____ _____

B. Answer true or false. Circle **T** for *true* or **F** for *false*.

1. Colcannon is a cold food.   T   F
2. Colcannon has three vegetables in it.   T   F
3. You cook the cabbage for colcannon.   T   F
4. You need some tomatoes for colcannon.   T   F
5. You need some salt for colcannon.   T   F

C. Write about a famous food from your country. What are the ingredients? How do you make it? When do people eat it?

_____

_____

_____

_____

_____

_____

_____

_____

_____

_____

Review

Solve the crossword puzzle with vocabulary and grammar from this unit.

Across

1. How _____ money do you have?
4. We have a _____ milk.
6. steak, chicken, and turkey
7. We have _____ popcorn.
10. milk, cheese, and butter (2 words)
11. he works in a restaurant
13. It's not important. It doesn't _____.
14. all the food you eat
15. I have _____ books. (2 words)
16. How _____ potatoes are there?

Down

2. a person who buys things
3. We have a _____ tomatoes.
5. tomatoes, onions, and potatoes
8. oranges, bananas, and apples
9. meat and fish
10. water, tea, and juice
12. Do you have _____ fruit?
16. Never _____. It's not important.

Lesson A

A. Unscramble the activities.

1. aprlingpel   r_____
2. bimcling   c_____
3. akgnit a krbea   t_____ a b_____
4. gsmiimwn   s_____
5. yiplang cesocr   p_____ s_____
6. gjgiogn   j_____
7. iflngti ghwtsei   l_____ w_____

B. Write questions and answers about the pictures. Use the present continuous tense.

1.
   a. **What are they doing now?**
   b. **They're cooking.**

2.
   a. _____.
   b. _____.

3.
   a. _____.
   b. _____.

4.
   a. _____.
   b. _____.

5.
   a. _____.
   b. _____.

6.
   a. _____.
   b. _____.

C. What are they doing now? Write sentences about friends and family members. Use your ideas and the present continuous tense.

1. **My brother is playing computer games.**
2. _____
3. _____
4. _____

Lesson B

A. Label the pictures with phrases from the box.

| watch a ball game | study | ice skate | fix the roof | play basketball | watch TV |

1. _____   2. _____   3. _____   4. _____   5. _____   6. _____

B. Today is a holiday. Look at these people's activities and write sentences with the simple present and present continuous tenses.

	Mondays	Today, Monday, May 1
Beth	clean her house	watch TV
Eric	go to his office	sleep late
Ms. Tyson	teach classes	swim at the Sports Center
Yuki and Yoko	study English	take a break
Mr. Kim	drive a bus	watch a ball game

1. (Beth) **On Mondays, Beth always cleans her house.** _____
   Today, she is watching TV. _____

2. (Eric) **On Mondays,** _____
   Today, _____

3. (Ms. Tyson) _____
   _____

4. (Yuki and Yoko) _____
   _____

5. (Mr. Kim) _____
   _____

C. Read the phone conversation. Write the verb in the simple present tense or the present continuous tense.

Jason: Hi, Rick. What are you doing?

Rick: Hi! You'll never guess. I (1) _____ (sit) in the living room at my parents' house.

Jason: Really? But you always (2) _____ (see) your cousin on Saturday.

Rick: Not today. He (3) _____ (work), so I (4) _____ (visit) my parents. We (5) _____ (look) at vacation photos and (6) _____ (talk about) their trip. And my mother (7) _____ (cook) dinner!

Lesson C

A. Write the sport that you play with these things.

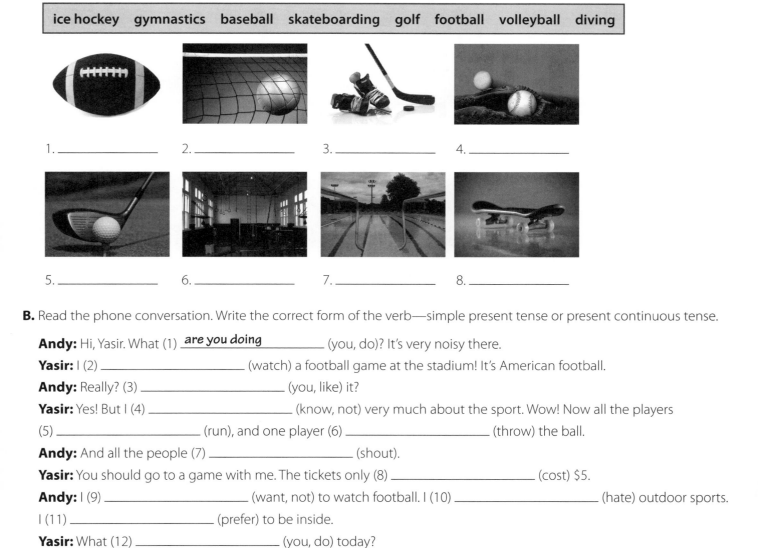

| ice hockey | gymnastics | baseball | skateboarding | golf | football | volleyball | diving |

1. _____   2. _____   3. _____   4. _____

5. _____   6. _____   7. _____   8. _____

B. Read the phone conversation. Write the correct form of the verb—simple present tense or present continuous tense.

Andy: Hi, Yasir. What (1) _are you doing_ (you, do)? It's very noisy there.

Yasir: I (2) _____ (watch) a football game at the stadium! It's American football.

Andy: Really? (3) _____ (you, like) it?

Yasir: Yes! But I (4) _____ (know, not) very much about the sport. Wow! Now all the players

(5) _____ (run), and one player (6) _____ (throw) the ball.

Andy: And all the people (7) _____ (shout).

Yasir: You should go to a game with me. The tickets only (8) _____ (cost) $5.

Andy: I (9) _____ (want, not) to watch football. I (10) _____ (hate) outdoor sports.

I (11) _____ (prefer) to be inside.

Yasir: What (12) _____ (you, do) today?

Andy: I (13) _____ (sit) in a chair and (14) _____ (listen) to the radio!

C. Answer the questions. Write complete sentences.

1. What sport do you like? Why? _____

_____

2. What sport do you hate? Why? _____

_____

Sports Around the World

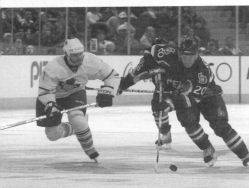

Soccer is very popular in Brazil. It's a great sport for people of all ages. You don't need much—just a ball and a place to play. You can play on a team, or you can just play with your friends. Soccer is popular in every country around the world. It's really an international sport.

I'm from Canada, and we love ice hockey here. It's very cold in winter, but we don't like to stay indoors. Our children play ice hockey at school. We watch their games and drink hot chocolate! Of course, we also watch famous hockey teams on TV.

The most popular sport in the United States is baseball. Some people think it's very slow, but it's a really interesting game. It's fun to sit outdoors with your friends at a baseball game. We eat chips and cheer for our team.

A lot of people in China play volleyball. We have teams at our schools and our offices. You can play volleyball indoors or outdoors. It's a good sport because you don't need expensive equipment. The only things you need are a ball and a net.

A. Complete the chart.

Country	Sport	Good things about the sport
Brazil		great for people _____ you need _____ and _____ it's _____ sport
	ice hockey	children play _____ people _____ at the games also watch _____
United States		it's _____, but it's _____ sit outdoors with _____ people eat _____ at the game
		teams at _____ and _____ can play _____ or _____ don't need _____

B. Write about a popular sport in your country. Who plays it? Who watches it? Do you like it? Why, or why not?

_____

_____

_____

_____

_____

_____

_____

_____

_____

Review

Solve the crossword puzzle with vocabulary and grammar from this unit.

Across

2. I'm tired, so I'm taking a _____.
3. On weekends I _____ ice skating.
5. We (cook) _____ dinner every day.
6. "I like basketball.""Me, _____."
7. You do this sport in a pool.
9. "I don't like tennis.""Me, _____."
13. not outdoor
15. Rock _____ is a dangerous sport.
16. I (study) _____ right now.
17. I (know) _____ a lot about sports.

Down

1. I lift _____ at the gym.
4. Baseball is a _____ sport. People do it together.
5. It's expensive. It _____ a lot of money.
8. Diving is an _____ sport. There are no teams.
10. things you need for a sport
11. He (prefer) _____ outdoor sports.
12. running
14. I like to _____ soccer.

Lesson A

A. Complete the expressions for vacation activities.

rent   take a   check in   take   visit   unpack   buy

1. _____ places of interest
2. _____ bus tour
3. _____ to the hotel
4. _____ a car
5. _____ photos
6. _____ your suitcases
7. _____ souvenirs

B. Write the past tense form of the verb. Be careful! Some verbs have *-ed* endings and some verbs are irregular.

1. see	saw	9. buy	
2. help		10. travel	
3. take		11. know	
4. ask		12. leave	
5. need		13. play	
6. fly		14. tell	
7. say		15. agree	
8. go		16. learn	

C. Look at the pictures and complete the conversation. Write questions and answers in the simple past tense.

Eric: Tell me about your vacation! (1) __Where did you go_____ (where/go)?

Ken: (2) _____ (we/go/India). It was great!

Eric: (3) _____ (where/fly to)?

Ken: (4) _____ (fly/New Delhi). We stayed for two nights.

(5) _____ (then/take/a train to Agra).

Eric: (6) _____ (what/do in Agra)?

Ken: (7) _____ (we/visit/the Taj Mahal). It was beautiful!

Eric: What about the food in India? (8) _____ (you/like it)?

Ken: Yes! (9) _____ (we/go/some great restaurants).

Lesson B

A. Read about the tour. Imagine you took the tour. Write sentences in the simple past tense.

A Week in Paris! Only $1995!

Monday	Leave home and fly to Paris. Go to the hotel.
Tuesday	Visit the Eiffel Tower.
Wednesday	See all the famous paintings in the Louvre Museum.
Thursday	Take a boat trip on the Seine River.
Friday	Watch artists in Montmartre and have dinner in a French restaurant.
Saturday	Go shopping at a famous department store and buy souvenirs.
Sunday	Go to the airport. Then return home.

1. On Monday, I left home and flew to Paris. I _____.

2. On Tuesday, I _____.

3. _____

4. _____

5. _____

6. _____

7. _____

B. Two people are talking about a vacation. Write the questions.

1. **Q:** _____?
   A: I went to Buenos Aires, in Argentina.

2. **Q:** _____?
   A: I stayed there for a week.

3. **Q:** _____?
   A: I visited all the famous places and ate great steaks.

4. **Q:** _____?
   A: I bought a cool jacket.

5. **Q:** _____?
   A: Yes, I really enjoyed it! It's a beautiful city!

Lesson C

A. Complete the sentences with the emphatic adjectives from the box. Use each word once.

horrible huge filthy fascinating excellent spotless exhausting

1. The museum was good. In fact, I think it was __excellent__.
2. The books were interesting. In fact, I think they were _____.
3. The food in the restaurant was bad. In fact, I think it was _____.
4. My hotel room was very clean. In fact, I think it was _____.
5. The trip was really tiring. In fact, I think it was _____.
6. The beaches were very dirty. In fact, I think they were _____.
7. The store was very big. In fact, I think it was _____.

B. Complete the sentences with your own ideas.

1. _____ is fascinating.
2. _____ are amazing.
3. _____ is awful.
4. _____ is wonderful.
5. _____ are horrible.
6. _____ is exhausting.

C. Complete the sentences with *was*, *wasn't*, *were*, and *weren't*.

1. Jacob __wasn't__ in class yesterday because he __was__ sick.
2. The stores _____ open last Monday because it _____ a holiday.
3. I didn't like my vacation. The hotel _____ horrible, and the restaurants _____ expensive.
4. I got 79 percent on that test. It _____ very long, and the questions _____ easy.
5. Where _____ you last night? I called you, but you _____ home.
6. I really liked that movie! The story _____ fascinating, and the actors _____ excellent.

D. Complete the conversations.

1.
A: _____ Alina at school yesterday?
B: No, she _____. She _____ at home.

2.
A: _____ you in Mexico on vacation?
B: No, _____. _____ in Brazil.

3.
A: _____ Rick at the sports center on Saturday?
B: No, _____. _____ at the library.

Lesson D

Hi Jess,

You asked about my vacation. There was good and bad.

It was a long trip. The airline was terrible. Everything was late, and the airplane was filthy with food on the floor and papers everywhere. We flew to the capital city, and then we took a train. We took a boat to get to White Beach. We left home at 5:00 a.m. and we arrived at 10:00 p.m.

The beach was amazing! It really is white, and it's very clean. In fact, it was spotless, and the water was warm and blue. We went swimming every day and walked on the beach. Our hotel was huge but very nice. The food was OK, but the restaurants had only a few different dishes. We had fish every day.

One day, we took a bus tour. It was exhausting! We went to about 20 different places. We only stayed for 10 minutes at each place, so we didn't have time to take photos. And the tour guide was terrible. He didn't speak English very well.

At the end of our vacation, we went to a gift shop. They had some nice souvenirs there. I bought t-shirts for all my friends. I have a t-shirt for you too!

See you soon!

Alia

A. Circle the correct answer.

1. Alia stayed at ___.

   a. the capital city   b. a beach   c. a small town

2. Her trip to White Beach was ___.

   a. easy   b. hard   c. short

3. The hotel was ___.

   a. big   b. dirty   c. fascinating

4. The food wasn't ___.

   a. healthy   b. interesting   c. delicious

B. What did Alia think about these things? Check ✓ her opinions.

	☺	😐	☹
1. her vacation			
2. the airplane			
3. the beach			
4. the hotel			
5. the food			
6. the bus tour			
7. the souvenirs			

C. You took a vacation in London. Look at the vacation information. Write a letter to your friend about it.

<u>Your London Tour</u>

- fly to Heathrow Airport
- five days in a big hotel
- eat in English restaurants
- visit the Tower of London
- see Buckingham Palace
- take a boat trip on the Thames River
- buy souvenirs in famous department stores

_____

_____

_____

_____

_____

_____

Review

Solve the crossword puzzle with vocabulary and grammar from this unit.

Across

3. past tense of *go*
5. I like to _____ photos.
6. very bad
8. I always _____ places of interest on vacation.
11. very big
12. very good
14. very clean
15. past tense of *see*
16. past tense of *say*
17. very dirty
18. very interesting

Down

1. past tense of *leave*
2. I always _____ a car to drive on vacation.
4. past tense of *fly*
7. very tiring
9. I always buy _____ to remember my vacation.
10. past tense of *take*
13. past tense of *buy*

Lesson A

A. Unscramble the ways to communicate.

1. ileam _____
2. xtte ssamege _____   _____
3. nepoh _____
4. axf _____

5. lteret _____
6. BlrykBacer _____
7. spnewerap da _____   _____

B. Which of the things in exercise **A** do you use? Who do you use them with?

_____

_____

C. Complete the sentences with indirect objects. Use object pronouns (*me, you, him, her, it, us, them*).

1. I'm hungry. Please give _____ a sandwich.
2. It's their anniversary. You should buy _____ a present.
3. I don't know his phone number. I'll send _____ an email.
4. My grandfather lives in Mexico. I write _____ a letter every month.
5. The horse is thirsty. Please give _____ some water.
6. You look bored. I'll tell _____ an interesting story.
7. We want to talk to you. Please give _____ a call.

D. Look at the people in the pictures. What will you do for them or give them for a present? Use indirect objects.

1.

I want to cook her a delicious dinner.

_____

2.

_____

_____

3.

_____

_____

4.

_____

_____

5.

_____

_____

Lesson B

A. Write the numbers in words.

1. 17 _seventeen_   7. 56 _____
2. 84 _____   8. 35 _____
3. 23 _____   9. 68 _____
4. 90 _____   10. 18 _____
5. 41 _____   11. 70 _____
6. 12 _____   12. 43 _____

B. Complete the sentences with words from the box.

phone number   mailing address   email address

1. My _____ is rita at coolmail dot com.
2. My _____ is area code eight-one-eight, five-five-five, nine-oh-one-two.
3. My _____ is four-thirty-three Russell Road, Middletown, postal code four-eight-seven-two-eight.

C. Complete the address book. Write the information in words.

YOU	YOUR FRIEND	YOUR FAMILY MEMBER
Name: _____	Name: _____	Name: _____
1. My phone number is	1. His/her phone number is	1. His/her phone number is
_____	_____	_____
2. My mailing address is	2. His/her mailing address is	2. His/her mailing address is
_____	_____	_____
_____	_____	_____
_____	_____	_____
3. My email address is	3. His/her email address is	3. His/her email address is
_____	_____	_____
_____	_____	_____

Lesson C

A. Write the sense for each picture.

| sight | taste | hearing | touch | smell |

1. _____ 2. _____ 3._____ 4. _____ 5. _____

B. Match the sentence parts.

1. That fish is old. It smells ___   a. sweet.
2. I like this jacket because it feels so ___   b. loud.
3. I don't like potato chips. They taste too ___ c. soft.
4. I washed my clothes this morning. Now they feel ___ d. salty.
5. Don't wear those jeans. They look ___   e. wet.
6. My brother plays a drum. It sounds very___ f. dirty.
7. You shouldn't eat those apples. They look too ___ g. bad.
8. I love chocolate because it tastes ___   h. green.

C. Circle the correct verb.

1. Can you hear that? My computer (sounds/looks) strange.
2. I like Thai food because it (feels/tastes) spicy.
3. Your new sunglasses (look/taste) really cool. Where did you get them?
4. My uncle gave me some perfume. It (looks/smells) like flowers.
5. The water (feels/sounds) really cold. I don't want to go swimming.
6. That camera (smells/looks) expensive. How much does it cost?

D. Complete the sentences. Use your ideas.

1. (taste) I like _____ because it tastes _____.
2. (smell) I don't like _____ because _____.
3. (feel) _____.
4. (look) _____.
5. (sound) _____.

▲ **a bee**

▲ **a wolf**

How Do Animals Communicate?

*A*nimals communicate in many different ways. Some animals use their whole bodies. For example, bees dance to communicate. They send messages about flowers and other places with food. Other bees see the dance and find the food.

Some insects communicate with smells. They make chemicals so that other insects can find them. Wolves and dogs also use smell to get a lot of information about other animals. And cats like to rub their bodies on things like trees to put their smell on them. The smell means, "This tree is mine!"

Many animals communicate by touching. For example, chimpanzees say "hello" by touching another chimpanzee's hand. When two horses put their noses together, it means, "We are friends."

And of course, many animals communicate with sounds. Birds use their beautiful songs to communicate. Dogs, cats, and people all make many different kinds of sounds, with different messages.

▲ **an insect**

▲ **a chimpanzee**

▲ **a bird**

▲ **a cat**

A. Write the names of the animals from the reading.

They hear messages.
They see messages.
They smell messages.
They touch messages.

B. Complete the sentences.

1. Bees dance to tell other bees about _____.
2. Insects use _____ to find other insects.
3. _____ like to put their smell on things.
4. Horses use their noses to communicate that they are _____.
5. People and birds both use _____ to communicate.

C. Write about ways to communicate with your friends. Which ways do you like the most? Why?

_____

_____

_____

_____

_____

_____

Review

Solve the crossword puzzle with vocabulary and grammar from this unit.

Across

5. past tense of *buy*
7. I wrote him a short _____ message.
8. French fries _____ salty.
10. Drums _____ loud.
14. I want to write you a letter. Please give me your _____ address.
15. I wrote to my mother. I sent _____ a letter.
17. I made a _____ call.
18. Those photos _____ interesting.

Down

1. past tense of *send*
2. past tense of *write*
3. past tense of *find*
4. past tense of *get*
6. This sense uses your ears.
9. This sense uses your hands.
11. Flowers _____ sweet.
12. It's his graduation. I sent _____ a card.
13. This sense uses your eyes.
16. These sweaters _____ soft.

Lesson A

A. Match the columns to make activities.

1. study ___
2. get ___
3. clean ___
4. buy a new ___
5. speak ___
6. do ___
7. have ___
8. buy my ___

a. car
b. own house
c. the house
d. English fluently
e. children
f. a new job
g. the laundry
h. for a test

B. Look at the information and write sentences about plans. Use *going to*. ✓ = yes ✗ = no

1. take a trip ✓
2. stay home ✗
3. pack their suitcases ✓
4. go to the airport late ✗

5. take an important test ✓
6. study very hard ✓
7. play computer games ✗
8. see his friends ✗

1. **They're going to take a trip.** _____
2. _____
3. _____
4. _____

5. _____
6. _____
7. _____
8. _____

C. Write the questions. Use *going to* and a question word from the box.

| who | what | where | when |

1. **A:** _____?
   B: I'm going to have pizza for dinner.

2. **A:** _____?
   B: They're going to be in the library.

3. **A:** _____?
   B: She's going to leave at ten o'clock.

4. **A:** _____?
   B: Our teacher is going to help me.

Lesson B

A. What are these people going to do? Write sentences.

1. He has a test tomorrow. <u>He's going to study.</u>
2. The children are very dirty. _____
3. I didn't eat breakfast, and now I'm hungry. _____
4. I don't have any food in my refrigerator. _____
5. There's a good programme on TV tonight. _____
6 My friend Annie's graduation is on Friday. _____

B. A reporter is interviewing you. Write the reporter's questions. Then write your answers.

1. (what/do tonight) <u>**What are you going to do tonight?**</u>

   Answer: _____

2. (do anything special/this weekend) _____?

   Answer: _____

3. (what/do Friday) _____?

   Answer: _____

4. (who/see this weekend) _____?

   Answer: _____

5. (what/watch on TV) _____?

   Answer: _____

6. (spend time with your family) _____?

   Answer: _____

7. (study English/this weekend) _____?

   Answer: _____

C. Write sentences about three of your short-term plans (this week).

1. _____
2. _____
3. _____

D. Write sentences about three of your long-term plans (one to five years).

1. _____
2. _____
3. _____

Lesson C

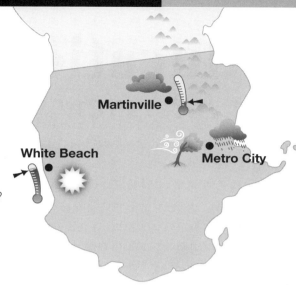

A. Look at the map. What are the weather predictions for the three cities?

1. In White Beach, it will be _____ and _____.
2. In Metro City, _____.
3. In Martinville, _____.

B. What clothes will people need tomorrow in the three cities in exercise **A**?
Write each thing in the correct box.

umbrella   rubber boots   scarf   raincoat
sunglasses   swimsuit   sunhat   sweater

White Beach	Metro City	Martinville

C. Write the conversation again. Change *going to* to *will*.

Kelly: Is it going to be warm on Saturday?

1. _____

Iman: No, it's going to be cold.

2. _____

Kelly: Then you're not going to have your graduation party outdoors.

3. _____

Iman: Of course we're going to be outdoors! We're going to wear sweaters and scarves.

4. _____
_____

D. Write predictions for the weather in your city. Use *will*.

1. tomorrow __It_____.
2. January _____.
3. July _____.
4. September _____.

Education for Tomorrow:
An Interview with Professor Angela Kwan

Professor Kwan, what are your predictions for education 20 years from now?

One big change will be the use of the Internet for education. People will use the Internet to take classes in many different subjects. For example, students will study a math or history lesson online, and then send their homework to the teacher by email. Students will attend famous universities in another country without leaving home.

These changes sound very exciting.

I also think we will spend more time studying. In the future, people will change their jobs many times. People will have three or four different jobs in their lives, and each time they'll go back to school for more training. So we'll see people of all different ages in colleges and technical schools.

What about the subjects children study in school? Will that change?

Yes, definitely. Children will use computers in school from the very beginning—at six years old. And foreign languages will be more important. All children will learn two or three languages in school—it's easy when you're young.

A. Which subjects does Professor Kwan make predictions about? Circle the correct answers.

homework	universities	classrooms	textbooks	computers
jobs	grades	lessons	tests	science classes

B. What does Professor Kwan think? Answer *Yes* or *No*.

1. The biggest change will be the cost of education.   Yes   No
2. Students will take classes over the Internet.   Yes   No
3. Students will mail their homework to their teacher.   Yes   No
4. People will spend less time studying.   Yes   No
5. People will keep the same job for their whole life.   Yes   No
6. People of different ages will go to school together.   Yes   No
7. Children will use computers when they are six years old.   Yes   No
8. Foreign languages won't be very important.   Yes   No

C. Write about your predictions for schools in the future. Write about the buildings, the teachers, the classes, the tests, and your other ideas.

_____

_____

_____

_____

_____

_____

_____

_____

Review

Solve the crossword puzzle with vocabulary and grammar from this unit.

Across

3. cloudy
5. I'm going to do the _____. I'm going to wash my clothes.
8. very cool
10. I'm _____ _____ study tonight. (2 words)
12. I wear _____ _____ on my feet in rainy weather. (2 words)
13. I wear a _____ to go swimming.
15. It's cold, so I'm wearing a _____.
18. It's rainy, so I'm wearing my _____.

Down

1. It will be sunny tomorrow. It _____ rain.
2. rainy
4. It's sunny. I need _____ for my eyes.
6. for a short time in the future
7. He speaks English very well! He speaks it _____.
9. It's raining. I'm using an _____.
11. for a long time in the future
14. It _____ be hot tomorrow.
16. breezy
17. very warm

SHOPPING FOR CLOTHES — UNIT 9

Lesson A

A. Label the clothes. Circle the ones you have.

gloves	**hat**	**slippers**	**flats**	**coat**	**stilettos**
pajamas	**sweater**	**scarf**	**loafers**	**robe**	**boots**

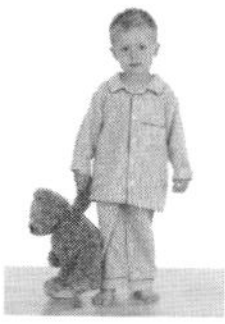

1. ______________

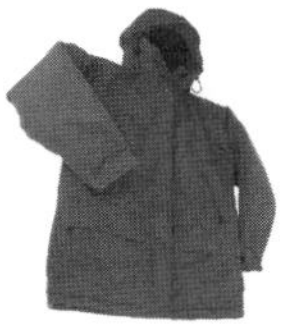

2. ______________

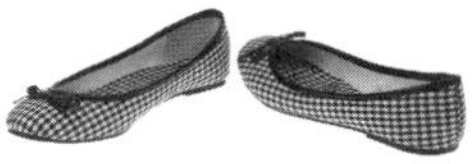

3. ______________

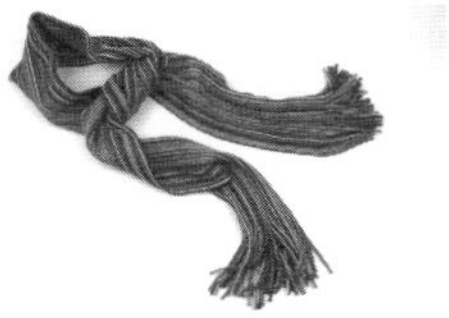

4. ______________

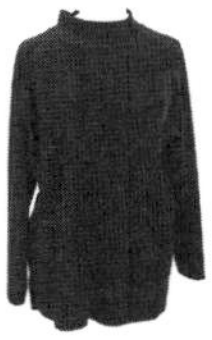

5. ______________

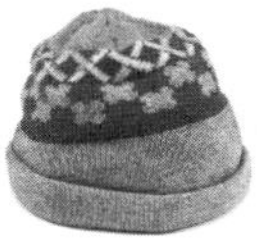

6. ______________

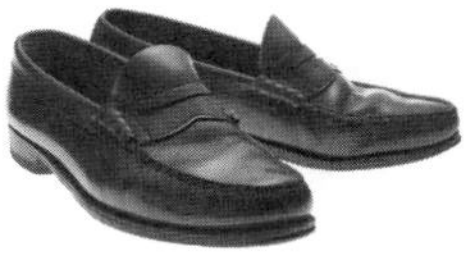

7. ______________

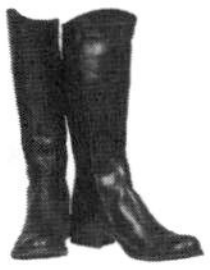

8. ______________

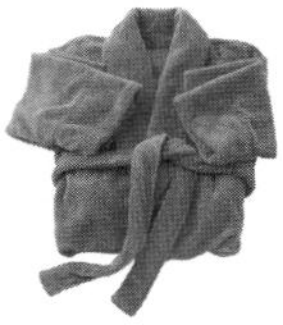

9. ______________

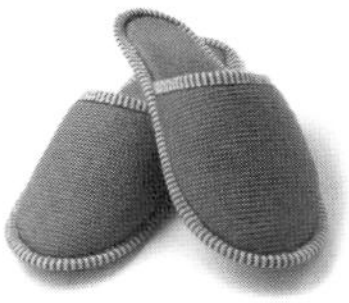

10. ______________

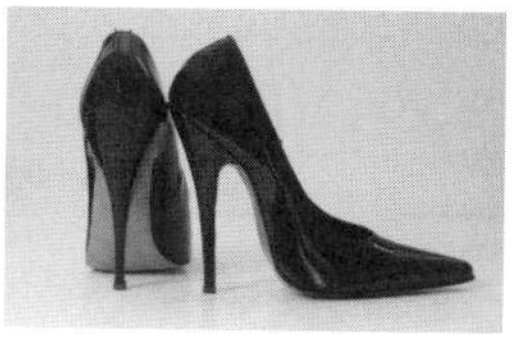

11. ______________

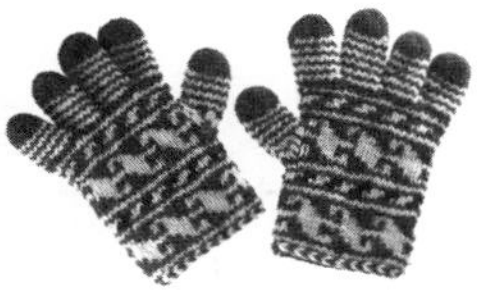

12. ______________

B. Write the opposite of the adjective.

1. old-fashioned ______________
2. expensive ______________
3. thin ______________
4. heavy ______________
5. casual ______________
6. poor quality ______________
7. machine-made ______________
8. warm ______________

C. Write sentences with comparative adjectives.

1. (this coat/warm/that coat) *This coat is warmer than that coat.*
2. (flats/comfortable/stilettos) ______________
3. (jeans/informal/a suit) ______________
4. (a raincoat/good/an umbrella) ______________
5. (a shirt/thin/a sweater) ______________
6. (this dress/pretty/that dress) ______________
7. (the black coat/cheap/the blue coat) ______________
8. (leather shoes/expensive/plastic shoes) ______________

Lesson B

A. Unscramble the questions in the conversation.

Sales clerk: (you can help I) (1) _____?

Ashley: Yes. I'd like a sweater to go with these pants.

Sales clerk: (what are you size) (2) _____?

Ashley: I'm a 16.

Sales clerk: (this what about sweater) (3) _____?

Ashley: It's very nice. (is it much how) (4) _____?

Sales clerk: It's $120.

Ashley: Hmmm . . . (anything do you expensive have a little less) (5) _____
_____?

Sales clerk: This one's on sale for $45.

Ashley: (can on I it try) (6) _____?

Sales clerk: Yes, the dressing rooms are over there.

B. Write the comparative adjective.

1. tall __taller__

2. easy _____

3. casual _____

4. large _____

5. interesting _____

6. handsome _____

7. bad _____

8. expensive _____

9. heavy _____

10. thin _____

11. warm _____

12. nice _____

C. Write sentences about your preferences. Use your own ideas and tell the reasons.

1. soccer/basketball/exciting __Basketball is more exciting than soccer because . . .__
   __or Soccer is more exciting than basketball because . . .__

2. shoes/boots/useful _____
   _____

3. emails/phone calls/good _____
   _____

4. jeans/a suit/nice _____
   _____

5. movies/TV/interesting _____
   _____

Lesson C

A. How do we take care of clothes? Label the pictures.

| bleach   iron   dry   wash   dry clean |

   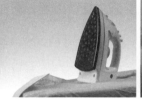 

1. _____ 2. _____ 3._____ 4. _____ 5. _____

B. Write examples of clothes made of these things.

cotton	leather	silk	wool	polyester
				coat
_____	_____	_____	_____	_____
_____	_____	_____	_____	_____

C. Complete the sentences with superlative adjectives.

1. English is _____ (easy) class at my school.
2. January is _____ (cold) month in my city.
3. Silk is _____ (expensive) material for clothes.
4. I think soccer is _____ (exciting) sport.
5. Summer is _____ (good) time to visit my country.
6. Jeans are _____ (comfortable) clothes to wear.
7. Plastic is _____ (bad) material for shoes. It's hot!

D. Write sentences with superlative adjectives. Use your ideas.

1. beautiful/place in our country

   I think _____

2. good/restaurant in our city

   _____

3. great/athlete in the world

   _____

4. interesting/program on TV now

   _____

5. big/problem in the world today

   _____

The Coolest T-Shirts in the World!

It's not just a boring t-shirt—It's a YOU-SHIRT! With you_shirts.com, you can have a t-shirt that fits your personality! You send us your information. We make your shirt. It's ready and at your house in just seven days!

A. Circle the correct answer.

1. What can you do on this Web site?

   a. see pictures of t-shirts   b. buy t-shirts   c. read about t-shirts

2. The t-shirts have _____ on them.

   a. words   b. designs   c. words and designs

3. _____ design the t-shirts.

   a. Artists   b. Students   c. Customers

4. There are _____ colors of t-shirts.

   a. three   b. four   c. six

5. You can get your t-shirt in _____.

   a. a day   b. a week   c. ten days

B. How much does each t-shirt cost? Read the Web site and find the total price.

1. An extra-large blue design t-shirt with extra-fast shipping.   Price: _____
2. A small yellow word t-shirt with ten words and regular shipping.   Price: _____
3. A medium black t-shirt with five words and a design, with regular shipping.   Price: _____
4. An extra-large green word and design t-shirt with eight words and extra-fast shipping.   Price: _____

C. Imagine you want to order a t-shirt. Fill out the Web page. How much will your t-shirt cost?

Price: _____

D. Write about the clothes you wear every day. Why do you like them?

_____

_____

_____

_____

_____

_____

_____

_____

_____

_____

Review

Solve the crossword puzzle with vocabulary and grammar from this unit.

Across

10. Jeans are made of ___.
11. wear these to sleep in
12. superlative of *beautiful*
14. comparative of *big*
16. comparative of *good*
17. not thin
18. wear these on your hands

Down

1. superlative of *good*
2. superlative of *nice*
3. superlative of *bad*
4. wear these on your feet in cold weather
5. not machine-made
6. not cheap
7. superlative of *pretty*
8. not formal
9. wear this on your head
13. wear these on your feet at home
15. the most expensive clothing material

Lesson A

A. Match the words and meanings.

 1. lifestyle __   a. not be strong and healthy

 2. be unfit __   b. exercise in a gym

 3. work out __   c. eat different kinds of healthy food

 4. be in good shape __   d. be strong and healthy

 5. junk food __   e. sitting in the sun

 6. sunbathing __   f. how you live

 7. eat a balanced diet __   g. unhealthy food like candy, chips, and cookies

B. How strong are these sentences? Circle the correct answer.

 1. You should go to bed earlier.

   suggestion   advice   obligation

 2. You have to quit smoking.

   suggestion   advice   obligation

 3. You could eat salad for lunch.

   suggestion   advice   obligation

 4. You ought to go to the gym after work.

   suggestion   advice   obligation

 5. You must stop eating sugar.

   suggestion   advice   obligation

 6. You shouldn't drink so much coffee.

   suggestion   advice   obligation

C. What would you say to these people?

 1. Your sister never eats vegetables. _____

 2. Your friend wants to get more exercise. _____

 3. Your little brother drinks soda for breakfast. _____

 4. Your father is always tired. _____

 5. Your mother wants to lose weight. _____

D. Think about a friend. Write health advice for your friend.

 Friend's name: _____

 1. _____

 2. _____

 3. _____

Lesson B

A. Complete the chart with the verbs. Then mark each habit as healthy or unhealthy.

lose	go	get	watch	work	eat	drink

	Healthy	Unhealthy
1. _____ to bed very late.		
2. _____ exercise every day.		
3. _____ a balanced diet.		
4. _____ weight.		
5. _____ out at a gym.		
6. _____ lots of soda.		
7. _____ less TV.		

B. You are a doctor. Write sentences for these people about their habits.

1. a. (should) **You should** _____.

   b. (could) _____.

   c. (have to) _____.

   d. (ought to) _____.

   e. (must) _____.

2. a. (should) **You should** _____.

   b. (could) _____.

   c. (have to) _____.

   d. (ought to) _____.

   e. (must) _____.

3. a. (should) **You should** _____.

   b. (could) _____.

   c. (have to) _____.

   d. (ought to) _____.

   e. (must) _____.

Lesson C

A. Fill in the words to make compound adjectives that match the meaning (in parentheses).

worked   free   watering   made   calorie   warming   long

1. (delicious) mouth-_____
2. (not from a factory) home-_____
3. (makes you happy) heart-_____
4. (for your whole life) life-_____
5. (relaxing) stress-_____
6. (too busy) over-_____
7. (won't make you fat) low-_____

B. Unscramble the questions. Then write your answers.

1. (are how you old) _____?

    Answer: _____

2. (sisters how brothers and do many you have) _____

    _____?

    Answer: _____

3. (how study long you English will today) _____

    _____?

    Answer: _____

4. (how junk you food do much eat) _____?

    Answer: _____

5. (you how do exercise often) _____?

    Answer: _____

C. A reporter is interviewing a famous basketball player. Write questions with *How*.

Reporter: How (1) _____ play basketball?

Marcus: I play basketball six times a week. That's every day, from Monday to Saturday.

Reporter: (2) _____

Marcus: I play basketball for at least two hours.

Reporter: (3) _____

Marcus: Oh, I don't spend much time at home. I just go there to sleep.

Reporter: (4) _____

Marcus: I'm 23 years old.

Reporter: (5) _____

Marcus: There are five people in my family—my mother, my father, my two sisters, and me.

How Long Will You Live?

Everyone wants to live a long and healthy life. Today, many scientists are trying to find the habits that help people live longer. In 1970, some scientists talked to 7000 people in the United States and got information about their habits. Then they checked to see how long the people lived.

The scientists learned that the people with the longest lives did six things.

1. They ate breakfast every day.
2. They didn't eat snacks between meals.
3. They weren't too heavy or too thin.
4. They exercised regularly.
5. They slept seven to eight hours every night—not more, and not less.
6. They didn't smoke.

These habits made a big difference. People who did all of these things lived 12 years longer than people who did only one to three of the things.

How can you change your habits? The scientists say you should change slowly. Make one small change every week. You need about 21 days to make a new habit.

A. What does the article say about these habits? Circle *good*, *bad*, or *no information* (if the article doesn't say).

1. eating eggs and toast for breakfast every day	good	bad	no information
2. sleeping nine hours a night	good	bad	no information
3. going to the doctor every year	good	bad	no information
4. going for a walk after dinner every night	good	bad	no information
5. being very thin	good	bad	no information
6. sunbathing for a short time every day	good	bad	no information
7. eating fruit for snacks every day	good	bad	no information

B. Answer the questions.

1. How many of the six habits do you have? _____

2. Which of the habits do you think is the easiest to do? Why? _____
   _____
   _____

3. Which of the habits do you think is the hardest to do? Why? _____
   _____
   _____

C. Write about a habit that you want to change. How did you start this habit? Why do you want to change it? How can you change it?

_____

_____

_____

_____

_____

_____

_____

_____

Review

Solve the crossword puzzle with vocabulary and grammar from this unit.

Across

4. You _____ take a walk every day. That's my suggestion.
6. How _____ will you live?
8. all your life
9. exercise in the gym
11. relaxed, with no problems
13. make something better
14. You _____ stop smoking or you will get very sick!
15. How _____ do you go to the gym?
16. How _____ water do you drink?

Down

1. with too much work
2. I eat a _____ diet with many different kinds of food.
3. food like candy, ice cream, and french fries (2 words)
5. the way you live
7. We eat _____ vegetables from our garden.
10. not healthy or strong
12. You _____ eat more fruit. It's a good idea.
15. You _____ to get more exercise. That's my advice.
16. How _____ cigarettes does he smoke?

Lesson A

A. Complete the sentences with verbs from the box.

| pay | walk | vacuum | buy | iron | sweep | cut | put away |

1. I always _____ the bills on the last day of the month.
2. My brother likes to _____ the grass on Saturdays.
3. Please _____ the clothes. They're on the table now.
4. I usually _____ the groceries on my way home from work.
5. You should _____ your dog for an hour every day. Dogs need a lot of exercise.
6. I don't like to _____ my clothes, so sometimes they don't look very nice!
7. Don't _____ now. Your father is sleeping, and it's very noisy. You should _____ the floor instead.

B. Complete the chart.

Verb	Past participle	Verb	Past participle
1. eat	*eaten*	9. take	
2. win		10.	told
3. have		11.	paid
4.	met	12. drink	
5.	gone	13.	put
6. sweep		14. say	
7. be		15.	read
8.	bought	16. speak	

C. Look at the picture and complete the conversation. Use the present perfect tense.

Megan: I've got a great new DVD. Do you want to come over and watch it with me?
Ashley: I can't go out yet. I (1) _____ (finish, not) my chores.
Megan: (2) _____ (clean) the kitchen?
Ashley: Well, I (3) _____ (vacuum) the living room, but I (4) _____ (wash, not) the dishes. And I (5) _____ (sweep, not) the floor in the kitchen.
Megan: Oh, that's too bad.
Ashley: What about you? (6) _____ (you, do) your homework?
Megan: Yes, I (7) _____ (finish) it.
Ashley: Great! Then you can come here and help me with my chores. I (8) _____ (not, walk) the dog!

Lesson B

A. Read the ad. Write questions for the job interview. Use the present perfect tense.

The Grand Hotel is looking for a Director of International Guest Services. You will help our foreign guests to enjoy their time in our city.

Requirements:

1. college graduate
2. classes in business administration
3. experience working in hotels
4. travel in other countries
5. driver's license an advantage

1. _Have you graduated from college?_

2. _____

3. _____

4. _____

5. _____

B. Read about these people. Write sentences about their achievements with the present perfect tense.

Aliza Shaw
- graduate, Central College
- no classes in business administration
- worked at Pacific Hotel (secretary)
- lived in Italy (five years)
- no driver's license (failed test)

1. _She has graduated from college._
2. _____
3. _____
4. _____
5. _____

Dwayne Harris
- student at Eastern University (will graduate next month)
- major: business administration
- worked at Hotel Splendid (in restaurant)
- traveled in Japan, Korea, and China
- driver's license

6. _____
7. _____
8. _____
9. _____
10. _____

C. Who is the best person for the job? Explain your reasons.

_____

_____

_____

_____

Lesson C

A. Match the columns to make achievements.

1. graduate ___   a. your driving test
2. get ___   b. abroad
3. run ___   c. from high school
4. buy your ___   d. own car
5. pass ___   e. a house
6. travel ___   f. a marathon
7. buy ___   g. credit card
8. get a ___   h. a promotion

B. Circle the correct form of the verb—simple past tense or present perfect tense.

1. Sumi (traveled/has traveled) to Europe three times. Last year, she (went/have gone) to Spain.
2. Our class (finished/has finished) 10 units in *World English* so far.
3. The weather (was/has been) very cold last week.
4. David is a TV reporter. He (met/has met) many famous people.
5. I (know/have known) my best friend all my life.
6. Justin (started/has started) a new job in October.
7. Marcela is a famous writer. She (wrote/has written) ten books.
8. I (ate/have eaten) lunch at one o'clock.

C. Have you ever done these things? Write sentences with the present perfect tense and simple past tense.

1. eat Japanese food (what?)
   a. *I've eaten Japanese food. OR I've never eaten Japanese food.*
   b. *I ate sushi.*
2. graduate from high school (when?)
   a. _____
   b. _____
3. travel abroad (where?)
   a. _____
   b. _____
4. meet a famous person (who?)
   a. _____
   b. _____
5. watch a movie in English (which one?)
   a. _____
   b. _____
6. buy something expensive (what?)
   a. _____
   b. _____

Amazing Achievements:
Stephen Hawking

Stephen Hawking is one of the most famous scientists in the world today. He uses mathematics to study space and the universe. He has written several famous books. He wrote *A Brief History of Time* in 1988, and more than 9 million people have bought this book. Other scientists have called Hawking the greatest scientist in the world.

Hawking has faced terrible problems in his life. When he was 21, he got a serious disease called ALS. The disease quickly got worse, and soon he couldn't walk or speak. Now, he can move only his left hand. He uses a wheelchair with a motor to get around. He "talks" by typing words into a computer. The computer pronounces the words for him.

But for Hawking, his work is more important than his problems. He teaches at Cambridge University in England, and he gives lectures at other universities. He has written many important scientific papers and has won many prizes for his work. He has been on TV many times. He has traveled in countries around the world, and he has even traveled in space! In 2007, he went up on a special zero-gravity plane.

Hawking's achievements are truly amazing. Even though his body is in a wheelchair, his mind explores the universe.

A. Find the information in the article.

1. What is Stephen Hawking's job? _____

2. What health problem does he have? _____

3. How does he get around? _____

4. How does he communicate? _____

5. Where does he teach? _____

B. Complete the sentences about Hawking's achievements.

1. He has written _____.

2. Other scientists have called him _____.

3. He has _____ scientific papers.

4. He has won _____.

5. He has been _____.

6. He _____ around the world.

7. He has also traveled _____.

C. What things have you done to improve your English? Write about them.

_____

_____

_____

_____

_____

_____

_____

_____

_____

_____

_____

Review

Solve the crossword puzzle with vocabulary and grammar from this unit.

Across

2. I (go) __ to Mexico last year.
6. past participle of *speak*
7. I (see) __ that movie three times. (2 words)
9. In a __, you run very far.
11. At a job __, you answer lots of questions.
13. food that you buy at the store
15. He will __ from high school next year.
16. If you get a __ at work, you get a better job.

Down

1. I (have) __ lunch, so I'm not hungry now. (2 words)
3. past participle of *take*
4. past participle of *drink*
5. past participle of *be*
8. an important thing that you have done
10. Have you __ had Lebanese food?
12. past participle of *eat*
14. I have traveled __. I went to Africa.
15. past participle of *go*
16. past participle of *put*

Lesson A

A. Complete the sentences with the correct form of a word from the box.

budget income expenses overspend lend save borrow

1. Families with children have a lot of _____. They must pay for food, clothes, and education for their children.
2. You should make a _____. You should plan how to spend your money.
3. Can you _____ me $10? I don't have enough money to buy this DVD.
4. I want to buy a car. I'm going to _____ some money every month.
5. Cassie always _____ on clothes, and then she can't pay her bills.
6. Jason has a very good _____. He's a writer, and he gets a lot of money from his books.
7. Most people have to _____ money when they want to buy a house.

B. Fill in the verbs in the real conditional sentences.

1. If I (eat) _____ more vegetables, I (lose) _____ weight.
2. If you (lend) _____ money to Ruth, you (get, not) _____ it back!
3. You (learn) _____ a lot of new words if you (read) _____ English magazines.
4. You (get) _____ stronger if you (work out) _____ at the gym every day.
5. If I (buy) _____ a new cell phone, I (have, not) _____ money for my bills.
6. He (be, not) _____ able to buy a car if he (save, not) _____ his money.

C. Look at the pictures and write real conditional sentences.

1. (study hard/get a good grade)
2. (go to bed late/feel tired tomorrow)
3. (buy a new computer/ not have money for a vacation)
4. (not eat more/be very unhealthy)

_____   _____   _____   _____

_____   _____   _____   _____

_____   _____   _____   _____

_____   _____   _____   _____

Lesson B

A. Jabir is a university student. Read his budget and answer the questions.

BUDGET: INCOME: $1000 A MONTH

Student apartment rent $350
Food at home $125
Food in restaurants $275
Transportation (taxi) $100
Textbooks $75
Cell phone $60
Going out with friends $200

TOTAL $1185

1. How much are his expenses every month? _____
2. What is his problem? _____
3. What are his three biggest expenses? _____

   _____

4. Which expenses can he change? _____

   _____

B. Jabir has made a list of things he can do to solve his problem. Write sentences about the consequences.

1. stay at home on Saturday night   4. take the bus
2. not eat in restaurants   5. learn how to cook
3. borrow money from brother   6. get a part-time job

1. **If he stays at home on Saturday night, he** _____.
2. _____.
3. _____.
4. _____.
5. _____.
6. _____.

C. What should Jabir do? Write advice for him. Use ideas from exercise **B** and your own ideas.

_____

_____

_____

Lesson C

A. Label the animals. Then write where each one lives.

orangutan shark mountain goat zebra camel	mountains grasslands coral reef rainforest desert

1. Animal: _____   2. Animal: _____   3. Animal: _____   4. Animal: _____   5. Animal: _____
   Habitat: _____   Habitat: _____   Habitat: _____   Habitat: _____   Habitat: _____

B. Think about the consequences and write sentences with *If*.

1. ~~the earth gets warmer~~	you won't need a raincoat
2. you travel in the desert	zebras will have to live in zoos
3. we cut down the rainforests	~~coral reefs will die~~
4. people use the grasslands for farms	orangutans won't have a home
5. you go to the mountains	you will see mountain goats

1. *If the earth gets warmer, coral reefs will die.*
   _____.
2. _____.
3. _____.
4. _____.
5. _____.

C. Rewrite the sentences from exercise **B.** Put *if* in the middle.

1. *Coral reefs will die if the earth gets warmer.*
   _____.
2. _____.
3. _____.
4. _____.
5. _____.

D. Complete the real conditional sentences. Use your own ideas.

1. If I overspend, _____.
2. If we don't stop pollution, _____.
3. _____, my English will improve.
4. _____, our teacher will be really happy.
5. _____, my family will worry.

http://www.naturevacationinc.com

Enjoy a Nature Vacation!
Our company has big plans for the future.

Featured Vacations...

- Featured Vacations
- Book a Vacation
- Search Hotels
- Search Major Cities
- Contact a Travel Agent
- Check your Scheduled Vacation Status

Rainforest Hotel

The building will be very tall so that 200 guests can see the tops of the trees. There will be nature programs about the plants and animals of the rainforest. A restaurant will serve dishes made from rainforest plants, and a shop will sell rainforest products. People will fly to a new airport near the hotel, so we won't need roads through the rainforest.

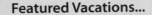

Coral Reef Ship

About 500 people will be on this ship. Tour guides will take guests swimming on the coral reefs. They can see fish and beautiful coral. On the ship, there will be information about preserving the coral reefs, and scientists will teach classes about saving the environment. Guests can eat coral reef fish in the ship's restaurant.

Mountain Camp

People will walk to this camp, high in the beautiful mountains. About 30 people will stay in the camp, and every day they will go walking in small groups. Tour guides will teach them about the animals in the mountains. Guests will sleep in small buildings made from local trees, and they will carry all their garbage home with them.

Opening next year! Click **here** for more information.

SITE MAP | CONTACT US | NEWSLETTERS | SUBSCRIPTION SERVICES | ADVERTISERS

A. Which place is it? Circle all the correct answers.

1. Guests will learn about the environment.

   Rainforest Hotel   Coral Reef Ship   Mountain Camp

2. People will see fish.

   Rainforest Hotel   Coral Reef Ship   Mountain Camp

3. It will be very large.

   Rainforest Hotel   Coral Reef Ship   Mountain Camp

4. Guests will go walking.

   Rainforest Hotel   Coral Reef Ship   Mountain Camp

5. People will eat food from that place.

   Rainforest Hotel   Coral Reef Ship   Mountain Camp

B. Which of these places is the WORST for the environment? Explain your answer. Use sentences with *if* to talk about consequences.

_____

_____

_____

_____

_____

_____

C. Which of these places is the BEST for the environment? Explain your answer. Use sentences with *if* to talk about consequences.

_____

_____

_____

_____

_____

_____

_____

_____

Review

Solve the crossword puzzle with vocabulary and grammar from this unit.

Across

3. keep your money to use in the future
4. give money that the other person will give back to you
5. If you study hard, you ___ pass the test.
7. result
14. a place with a lot of grass
15. a big fish with dangerous teeth
16. deciding something
18. ways to go to another place

Down

1. spend too much
2. a place in the ocean with coral and many fish (2 words)
6. all the money you get
8. things you must pay
9. the place where an animal usually lives
10. get money that you must give back
11. a plan for spending money
12. very dry land
13. a black and white animal
17. ___ you buy a car, you won't have money for your vacation.

VOCABULARY INDEX

airline ticket ....U 3
airport ....U 3
alternatives ....U 8
amazing ....U 6
animals ....U 12
apples ....U 4
aquarium ....U 7
Australia ....U 1
Australian ....U 1
awful ....U 6
bad ....U 6
bad shape ....U 10
bagels ....U 4
Bahrain ....U 1
Bahraini ....U 1
baked beans ....U 4
bananas ....U 4
baseball ....U 5
big ....U 6
BlackBerry® ....U 7
board the airplane ....U 3
boots ....U 9
boring ....U 1
borrow ....U 12
bought ....U 11
breakfast cereal ....U 4
breezy ....U 8
bright ....U 8
broccoli ....U 4
budget ....U 12
butter ....U 4
buy a new car ....U 8
buy a house ....U 11
buy duty free goods ....U 3
buy my own house ....U 8
buy souvenirs ....U 6
buy the groceries ....U 11
buy your own car ....U 11
buy your ticket ....U 3
camel ....U 12
cash ....U 3
casual ....U 9
catch the bus ....U 2
cauliflower ....U 4
celebrate ....U 2
cheap ....U 9
check in ....U 3
check into the hotel ....U 6
checks ....U 3

cheese ....U 4
chicken ....U 4
claim your baggage ....U 3
clap ....U 7
clean ....U 6
clean the house ....U 8
climbing ....U 5
cloudy ....U 8
clutch ....U 9
cocoon ....U 9
coffee ....U 4
cold ....U 8
commerce ....U 9
cool ....U 8
coral reef ....U 12
cost-effective ....U 8
costumes ....U 2
countries ....U 1
credit cards ....U 3
cut the grass ....U 11
cycling ....U 10
dairy products ....U 4
dangerous ....U 1
decorate ....U 2
desert ....U 12
difficult ....U 1
dirty ....U 6
disappointing ....U 12
diving ....U 5
do the laundry ....U 8
doctor ....U 1
documents ....U 3
dolphin speak ....U 7
draining ....U 12
drinking lots of water ....U 10
drinks ....U 4
drunk ....U 11
dull ....U 8
easy ....U 1
eat breakfast ....U 2
eat out ....U 2
eaten ....U 11
eating a balanced diet ..U 10
eating lots of sugar ....U 10
eggs ....U 4
email ....U 7
engineer ....U 1
enormous ....U 6
excellent ....U 6

exhausting ....U 6
expenses ....U 12
expensive ....U 9
expiration date ....U 3
fascinating ....U 6
fashionable ....U 9
fax ....U 7
feast ....U 2
festivals ....U 2
filthy ....U 6
fireworks ....U 2
fish ....U 4
fit ....U 6
fix the roof ....U 5
flats ....U 9
floating village ....U 5
football ....U 5
formal ....U 9
fortress ....U 6
France ....U 1
French ....U 1
fruit ....U 4
fun ....U 2
genes ....U 10
get a credit card ....U 11
get a new job ....U 8
get promotion ....U 11
get up ....U 2
getting eight hours
    sleep every night ....U 10
gloves ....U 9
go ice skating ....U 5
go through customs ......U 3
go through
    immigration ....U 3
go through security ....U 3
go to a ball game ....U 5
go to bed ....U 2
go to the movies ....U 2
golf ....U 5
good ....U 6
good shape ....U 10
good-bye ....U 7
gorge ....U 6
graduate from high
    school/university ....U 11
grasslands ....U 12
green ....U 7
gymnastics ....U 5

habitats ....U 12
handbag ....U 9
handmade ....U 9
happy ....U 1
hard ....U 9
hat ....U 9
have children ....U 8
healthy ....U 10
hearing ....U 7
heart-warming ....U 10
heavy ....U 9
hello ....U 7
homegrown ....U 10
homemade ....U 10
horrible ....U 6
hot ....U 8
huge ....U 6
ice hockey ....U 5
income ....U 12
informal ....U 9
interesting ....U 1
international driver's
    license ....U 3
Ireland ....U 1
Irish ....U 1
iron the clothes ....U 11
jogging ....U 5
jokes ....U 10
Jordan ....U 1
Jordanian ....U 1
juice ....U 4
junk food ....U 10
ladders ....U 6
lemons ....U 4
lend ....U 12
letter ....U 7
lettuce ....U 4
lifelong ....U 10
lifestyle ....U 10
lifting weights ....U 5
light ....U 9
loafers ....U 9
looking for ....U 5
looms ....U 9
loud ....U 7
low-calorie ....U 10
luxury ....U 4
machine made ....U 9
magnificent ....U 6

masks ....U 2
meat ....U 4
met ....U 11
Mexican ....U 1
Mexico ....U 1
milk ....U 4
modern ....U 9
mountain goat ....U 12
mountains ....U 12
mouth-watering ....U 10
nationalities ....U 1
newspaper ad ....U 7
nice ....U 6
nightgown ....U 9
nuts ....U 4
occupants ....U 6
occupations ....U 1
Okinawans ....U 10
old-fashioned ....U 9
onions ....U 4
oranges ....U 4
orangutan ....U 12
orbiting ....U 11
outstanding ....U 6
overcast ....U 8
overspend ....U 12
overworked ....U 10
pack your bags ....U 3
pack/unpack suitcase ....U 6
packing ....U 3
pajamas ....U 9
parka ....U 9
pass your driving test .....U 11
passport ....U 3
pay the bills ....U 11
peppers ....U 4
perfume ....U 10
Peru ....U 1
Peruvian ....U 1
phone ....U 7
photographer ....U 1
pilot ....U 1
play basketball ....U 5
playing soccer ....U 5
police officer ....U 1

poor ....U 1
potatoes ....U 4
presents ....U 2
prevent ....U 10
protein ....U 4
provide ....U 12
pumps ....U 9
put away the
  clothes ....U 11
quality ....U 9
raincoat ....U 8
rainforest ....U 12
rainy ....U 8
raise ....U 7
rappelling ....U 5
read ....U 11
read the newspaper ....U 2
recover ....U 12
renewable ....U 8
rent a car ....U 6
rich ....U 1
robe ....U 9
rough ....U 9
rubber boots ......U 8
run a marathon ....U 11
run away ....U 10
safe ....U 1
said ....U 11
salary ....U 1
salty ....U 7
Sambadrome ......U 2
sausages ....U 4
save ....U 12
say ....U 7
scarf ....U 9
shark ....U 12
sight ....U 7
skateboarding ....U 5
slippers ....U 9
smell ....U 7
smoking ....U 10
smooth ....U 9
soda ....U 4
soft ....U 7
solar system ....U 11

speak English fluently ....U 8
spin ....U 9
spoken ....U 11
spotless ....U 6
squid ....U 5
start work ....U 2
steak ....U 4
steel ....U 9
stilettos ....U 9
stop ....U 7
stress-free ....U 10
student loan ....U 12
study ....U 5
study for the next
  test ....U 8
sun hat ....U 8
sunbathing ....U 10
sunglasses ....U 8
sunny ....U 8
sweater ....U 8
sweep the floor ....U 11
sweet ....U 7
swept ....U 11
swimming ....U 5
swimsuit ....U 8
take a bus tour ....U 6
take a nap ....U 2
take a shower .....U 2
take a taxi ....U 3
take photos ....U 6
taking a break .....U 5
talk ....U 7
tanks ....U 7
taste ....U 7
tea ....U 4
teacher ....U 1
terrible ....U 6
text message ....U 7
Thai ....U 1
Thailand ....U 1
thick ....U 9
thin ....U 9
thread ....U 9
tie ....U 2
tiring ....U 6

to cost ....U 5
to hate ....U 5
to know ....U 5
to like ....U 5
to need ....U 5
to prefer ....U 5
to think ....U 5
to want ....U 5
told ....U 11
tomatoes ....U 4
tomb ....U 9
touch ....U 7
travel abroad ......U 11
travel agent ....U 1
travel insurance ....U 3
traveler's checks ....U 3
tropical forest .....U 6
trunks ....U 6
tuna salad ....U 4
TV ....U 7
ugly ....U 8
umbrella ....U 8
unfit ....U 10
unhappy ....U 1
unintentionally ....U 4
vacuum ....U 11
vegetables ....U 4
visa ....U 3
visit friends ....U 2
visit places of
  interest ....U 6
volleyball ....U 5
walk the dog ......U 11
warm ....U 8
watch TV ....U 2
watching too
  much TV ....U 10
water ....U 4
weaving ....U 9
wet ....U 7
wetlands ....U 12
windy ....U 8
won ....U 11
works out ....U 10
zebra ....U 12